Sanjeev Kapoor's

Tasty Eating
for Healthy Living

In association with Alyona Kapoor

- Volume One -

PopulaR
prakashan

www.popularprakashan.com

Published by:

POPULAR PRAKASHAN PVT. LTD.

301, Mahalaxmi Chambers

22, Bhulabhai Desai Road

Mumbai 400 026

for **KHANA KHAZANA PUBLICATIONS PVT. LTD.**

(4305)

ISBN – 978-81-7991-557-8

Nutritionist: Kirti Masurkar

Book Design: Pratibha Gurnani Creative

Photography: Bharat Bhirangi, Alim Bolar

Food Stylist: Anupa Das

Printed in India

Standard Press (India) Pvt. Ltd.,

34G, Poothayammal Nagar,

Near YRTV School, Sivakasi - 626 123.

author's note

This collection of recipes is for those who care about eating healthy and staying fit. With a proper diet and exercise any person can live well for a long, long time.

Human beings were designed as hunter-gatherers. They hunted food, and as natural food decays very rapidly, they consumed it immediately... ancient man ate to live, only enough to keep hunger at bay. Modern man's body has basically the same metabolic processes as our hunter-gatherer ancestors, but our lifestyle has changed dramatically.

We do hunt and gather... in the car till the supermarket, where we buy packaged processed foods which are usually stored in the refrigerator! While modern life has many conveniences, our bodies have been designed in an extraordinary manner, with significant reserves and safety mechanisms to ensure prolonged survival. But we are pushing these mechanisms to the limit with our modern 'convenient' lifestyle.

Modern living is a continuous battle to stay healthy, keep fit, cope with stress, maintain a normal weight, and ultimately, achieve longevity. Here a healthy diet plays a major role. *Tasty Eating for Healthy Living* is a collection of recipes from India and around the world that have been improvised and modified to make them suitable for our modern lifestyle, without sacrificing taste and nutrition.

We all love food. There is not only sustenance in it but also comfort. If there is good healthy food put on the table everyday, then you are on the right road to well-being. These recipes will help you make the best use of all the available natural and fresh ingredients to dish up great-tasting food and most important, healthy food!

All recipes are meant to serve four people keeping in mind there are other complementary dishes in the meal.

Eat healthy, live long!

Sanjeev Kapoor

contents

What is a Balanced Diet?   6

Soups

Mushroom Soup with Light Soy   15

Gazpacho   16

Chicken Noodle Soup   17

Chicken Barley Soup   18

French Onion and Garlic Soup   19

Tomato and Basil Soup   20

Mutton Pudina Shorba   21

About Healthy Foods   22

Snacks and Starters

Pan-fried Mushrooms   30

Quesadillas   31

Dilli Aloo Kachalu Chaat   32

Green Chana Chaat   33

Fruit Chaat   34

Peanut Chaat   35

Rajma Galouti Kababs   36

Hara Bhara Kabab   37

Masala Dosa Chaat   39

Dabeli   40

Masala Khichia Papad   41

Vegetable Seekh Kabab   42

Fish Tikka Achaari   43

Broken Wheat Upma   44

Makai, Badam aur Akhrot ki Tikki   45

Patra   46

Pav Bhaji Roll-Ups   48

Corn Bhel   49

Saunfia Paneer Tikka   51

Teriyaki Rolls   52

Paneer Tikka Kali Mirch   54

Tandoori Murgh Chaat   57

Paneer ke Tinke   58

Soya Burger   61

Kali Mirch Tikka   63

Sichuan Prawns   64

Boti Kabab   65

Spicy Moroccan Wraps   66

Shawarma   68

Tandoori Pomfret   69

Healthy Cornflakes Bhel   70

Aloo Anaardana Chaat   72

what is a balanced diet?

The human body requires food to provide energy for all life processes and for growth, repair and maintenance of cells and tissues. The dietetic needs vary according to age, sex and occupation. Every ingredient that we partake of has a specific role to play in our health. Eating a well-balanced diet on a regular basis and staying at an ideal weight are critical factors in maintaining emotional and physical well-being. The word 'diet' is often used to describe an eating plan intended to aid weight-loss. However, diet really refers to the foods a person eats in the course of a day, or a week. The more balanced and nutritious the diet, the healthier the person can expect to be. A balanced diet means eating the right amount of food from all the food groups. Choose the types of foods that improve your health and avoid the types of foods that raise your risk for illnesses such as heart disease and diabetes. Expand your range of healthy choices to include a variety of delicious foods.

The benefits of a balanced diet are numerous. No single food contains everything the body needs so it is important to eat a variety of them. The right amount of essential nutrients can increase life expectancy by keeping the heart and body healthy and preventing many long-term illnesses.

the concept of healthy eating

Healthy eating is based on three simple aspects - Balance, Moderation and Variety. When these three parameters are mastered, one feels great, has more energy and remains healthy! There are no strict nutrition philosophies, or a rule that one has to stay unrealistically thin. Healthy eating also does not mean that one is deprived of favourite foods. Learning some nutrition basics and incorporating them in a way that works for you can achieve all this. Believe it or not, healthy eating can be tasty, exciting and exotic too!

basics are essential

Every ingredient from the basic five food groups has a specific role to play in your health. That's why we should aim for a balanced diet. Eating too much of one or not enough of another is not good for anyone and may result in deficiencies.

A balanced diet contains different types of foods in those quantities and proportions such that the need for calories, proteins, minerals, vitamins and other nutrients is adequately met and a small provision is made for extra nutrients for when one's health comes under stress.

The different food groups that should be included in the diet so as to get the necessary nutrients are cereals and millets, pulses, fruits and vegetables, milk and milk products, meat and meat products, sugar and fat. In addition, a balanced diet should provide non-nutrients like fibre, which provides positive health benefits. Fluid intake in the form of water and water-based drinks is also essential for good health. Water is essential for the correct functioning of the kidneys and bowels. At least 6-8 glasses of plain water should be consumed each day.

food guide pyramid

A food guide pyramid is a simple way of knowing the kinds of food one needs to consume and in what amounts to ensure good health.

It is obvious that there is an interplay of nutrients in the body. When we talk about nutrients it is important to know the quantity i.e. how much to eat. This can be understood better with the concept of a **Food Guide Pyramid.** This can form a foundation for a good diet that provides the essential nutrients.

Definition of RDA

The Recommended Daily Allowance (RDA) is the amount of a particular nutrient that must be consumed daily to ensure good health. The RDA percentages are scientifically calculated and are accepted worldwide.

food guide pyramid (for vegetarians)

Food Groups

Cereals: Cereals form the staple diet in India e.g. rice, wheat, maize. Cereals generally lack lysine, however rice is richer in lysine compared to other cereals. Ragi, a millet, is a rich source of proteins and calcium and is known as poor man's milk. Cereals do not contain Vitamin A and Vitamin C except yellow maize, which contains carotene.
1 cereal serving = 1 *katori* of cooked rice or 2 *phulkas* or 2 slices of bread.
1 cereal serving will supply about 100 calories and 2-3 grams of protein.

Legumes (pulses and dals): Pulses are rich sources of protein (upto 22-25%). Vegetarians can meet their protein requirement by including different pulses in their diet. But they lack Vitamin A and Vitamin C. However, germination of pulses increases the Vitamin C levels. Soaking and cooking of legumes destroy their anti-nutritional factors like tannin and trypsin inhibitors and make them easier to digest. Cereal-pulse combination in a proportion of 4:1 or 3:1 is enough for its supplementary effect.
1 serving of legumes = 1 *katori* of cooked *dal* or pulses
1 serving of legumes = 100 calories and 6-7 grams proteins.

Vegetables: Green leafy vegetables are very rich sources of Vitamin B, carotene, iron, calcium, Vitamin B complex and Vitamin C. At least fifty grams should be consumed daily by everyone. Yellow-orange vegetables are good sources of Vitamin B, carotene, and lycopenes. Roots and tubers are rich in carbohydrates and contain some vitamins and minerals. Three to five servings of vegetables per day are a must and one of them should be a green leafy vegetable.

Fruits: They are a rich source of vitamins, minerals and fibres. Green, yellow and orange fruits like mango and papaya contains beta-carotene. *Amla*, citrus fruits and guava are a rich source of Vitamin C. Dried fruits like dates supply iron. Banana and jackfruit are good sources of energy. Two to three servings of fruits per day are recommended.

Milk and milk products: Milk is a good source of protein, calcium and vitamins. It is deficient in iron and Vitamin C. Whole milk has a high percentage of fat (8-12%) whereas low-fat or toned milk has about three percent fat. Skimmed milk has very little or no fat. Two to three servings per day are recommended, where one serving = 1 cup (225-240 ml).

food guide pyramid (for non-vegetarians)

Food Groups

Meat/Fish/Poultry: Egg, fish, meat etc. are included in this group. Eggs supply good-quality protein, vitamins and fat. Fish, meat and chicken are good sources of protein and vitamins. Meat has more fat as compared to poultry and fish. Omega 3-PUFA in fish protects against cardiovascular diseases. Two to three servings/day are recommended.

One serving has about 30 grams of cooked meat.
One serving provides 100 calories and 7 grams of protein.

Fat/Oils: Calories from fat should not exceed 10-15% of the total calorie intake. Fat is made use of not only during cooking (visible source) but it is also present within the food we eat such as seeds, nuts, pulses etc. Fifteen to twenty grams of visible fat (oil/ghee) is recommended per person per day.

One gram of oil or ghee gives 9 calories.
One teaspoon of ghee, butter, oil = 45 calories.

Sugars: This group includes sugar, honey, jaggery, etc., which are concentrated sources of energy. Jaggery provides a little iron. This group has to be used sparingly. Excessive intake of sugars is not desirable as it leads to wide fluctuations in blood sugar levels and obesity.

1 teaspoon sugar = 20-25 calories.

balanced diet vs. healthy diet

That a balanced diet is better for health is an accepted fact but some believe a healthy diet also means a balanced diet. In fact they are both different. The difference is a healthy diet plan provides us withsome nutrients but a balanced diet plan provides us with all the essential nutrients.
A balanced diet enables us to obtain all the essential nutrients present in a wide range of foods. If the balanced diet plan is consistent it will also provide a regular supply of vitamins, minerals and other essential nutrients ensuring optimum health and vitality. Optimum health means fewer illnesses and health complications but more importantly increased energy levels for physical activity. It also helps in weight-loss.

It's important to be aware that a balanced diet can also provide too many fats, refined sugar and salt. If any diet provides excessive saturated fats, cholesterol and refined sugars it may be classed as unhealthy. This is where Healthy Diet comes in. A Healthy Diet Plan is mainly the consumption of natural, fresh and wholesome foods for each meal of the day; foods chosen are usually low in fats, sodium and refined sugars.

The idea of combining both the healthy and balanced diet plans is to provide a variety in the diet, to consume more whole grains, *dals*, pulses, sprouts, fresh fruits and vegetables which help in boosting the energy level. This combination focuses on a low fat intake especially saturated fats and minimizes refined sugar and salt intake. The underlying principle is to provide optimum health and vitality, to have more energy to be more active and to build up stamina.

choosing the right foods

Nutrients in food perform various essential functions. They help in body-building, growth, giving energy and provide protection. The various foods categorized as nutrients perform specific functions in our body, so to maintain a balance is of utmost importance. The classification of foods as per their functions helps one decide on the right kind of foods.

• ***Energy-giving foods***
Simple carbohydrates: sugars, honey, jaggery
Fats and oils

• ***Body-building foods***
Proteins
Complex carbohydrates

• ***Protective foods***
Vitamins
Minerals

oups

mushroom soup with light soy

Ingredients

4-5 medium fresh button mushrooms
1 teaspoon light soy sauce
3 cups Vegetable Stock (Vol. 5, page 66)
150 grams silken tofu, finely diced
Salt to taste
½ teaspoon black pepper powder
4 teaspoons sliced spring onions

Method

❶ Bring the vegetable stock and light soy sauce to a boil in a deep pan.

❷ Add the mushrooms and tofu and cook on low heat for three to four minutes but do not allow the mixture to boil. Add the salt and pepper powder. Stir to mix well.

❸ Transfer into individual soup bowls, sprinkle a teaspoon of chopped spring onions on each and serve piping hot.

Healthy and rich in protein, this soup can be prepared in a jiffy! Mushrooms and tofu hardly take any time to cook. This recipe has multi-nutrients and is recommended for all age groups.

gazpacho

Ingredients

2-3 slices brown bread
3-4 garlic cloves, coarsely chopped
6 medium tomatoes, quartered
1 medium cucumber, seeded and
roughly chopped
1 medium green capsicum,
roughly chopped
Salt to taste
2 tablespoons wine vinegar
2 tablespoons olive oil

Garnish
1 small onion, chopped
1 small green capsicum, chopped
1 slice white bread, cut into
½-inch cubes

Method

❶ Soak the bread in half a cup of water for five minutes and squeeze out excess water.

❷ Process the bread with the garlic, tomatoes, cucumber and chilled water in a blender.

❸ Add the capsicum and salt and process again.

❹ Add the wine vinegar and olive oil and continue to process.

❺ Strain the soup into a bowl and chill in a refrigerator.

❻ Garnish with the onion, green capsicum and bread cubes. Serve chilled.

Chef's Tip: You can use malt vinegar or lemon juice instead of wine vinegar.

Gazpacho, the famed cold soup from Spain, is fondly called chunky liquid salad at home! Have it on a hot summer day. The brown bread is my idea for increasing the fibre in the soup. Gazpacho is rich in Vitamin C, low in calories and trans-fats and the garlic and olive oil help in lowering cholesterol levels.

chicken noodle soup

Ingredients

300 grams rice noodles or rice vermicelli
2 fresh red chillies, seeded and sliced
2 tablespoons soy sauce
1¼ cups bean sprouts, blanched
1 medium onion, sliced
White pepper powder to taste
2 tablespoons chopped fresh coriander
10-12 fresh basil leaves
1 lemon, cut into wedges

Broth

10 cups Chicken Stock (Vol. 5, page 66)
500 grams boneless chicken, skinned
 and cubed
1 inch cinnamon
4 spring onions, sliced
1 inch ginger, crushed
2 teaspoons sugar
Salt to taste
2 tablespoons fish sauce

Method

❶ Place the sliced red chillies in a bowl and add the soy sauce. Set aside.

❷ For the broth, bring the chicken stock, chicken, cinnamon, spring onions, ginger, sugar and salt to a boil over high heat in a deep pan. Reduce heat and simmer for forty-five minutes, skimming off the scum as it rises to the surface.

❸ Add the fish sauce and remove from heat. Remove the chicken and set aside to cool. Strain the mixture and keep the clear broth warm over very low heat.

❹ Boil plenty of water in a deep pan, add the noodles and blanch for about five minutes or until they soften. If using vermicelli it will take around two minutes. Drain and rinse in cold water. Drain thoroughly and set aside.

❺ When the chicken cools down, shred it into thin strips.

❻ Place the noodles/vermicelli in individual serving bowls, top with the bean sprouts, shredded chicken and onion. Pour the hot broth over. Sprinkle the white pepper powder and serve piping hot garnished with fresh coriander and basil leaves along with lemon wedges and the bowl of red chillies in soy sauce.

This soup is excellent for growing kids what with the protein-rich bean sprouts and chicken!

chicken barley soup

Ingredients

2 chicken legs, skinned
½ cup barley
1 bay leaf
4-6 black peppercorns
2 medium carrots, cut into fingers
1 medium onion, sliced
3-inch celery stalk, cut into 1-inch pieces
2 tablespoons butter
Salt to taste
¼ teaspoon white pepper powder
½ tablespoon cornflour
1 tablespoon chopped fresh parsley
1 small cucumber, seeded and cubed

Method

❶ Soak the barley in two cups of water for an hour.

❷ Take seven cups of water in a heavy-bottomed pan and add the bay leaf, peppercorns, carrots, onion, celery and chicken to it. Bring it to a boil and lower the heat.

❸ Continue to simmer on medium heat, removing the scum from time to time. Cook for thirty to thirty five minutes on medium heat.

❹ Strain the stock and set it aside. Debone the chicken legs and chop the meat. Discard the vegetables.

❺ Drain the water from the soaked barley.

❻ Melt the butter in a non-stick pan on low heat, add the barley and cook for three to four minutes.

❼ Add the reserved stock and continue cooking for another half an hour.

❽ Add the salt and white pepper powder.

❾ Add the chicken to the barley mixture and simmer for another three to four minutes.

❿ Add the cornflour dissolved in half cup of water, cook for a minute and remove from heat. Add the parsley and stir.

⓫ Serve piping hot garnished with cubes of cucumber.

My daughters love chicken and I have added barley to increase the fibre content. The carrots and celery add Vitamins A and C. An ideal soup for the whole family as it gives instant energy.

french onion and garlic soup

Ingredients

3 medium onions, thinly sliced
5-6 garlic cloves
4 slices brown bread
2 tablespoons olive oil
1 medium carrot, thinly sliced
4 cups Vegetable Stock (Vol. 5, page 66)
Salt to taste
¼ teaspoon white pepper powder
¼ cup grated cheese

Method

❶ Chop three to four garlic cloves and keep the remaining whole.

❷ Cut the brown bread into small round slices. Apply one tablespoon olive oil and rub with whole garlic cloves. Toast till crisp.

❸ Heat the remaining olive oil in a non-stick pan, and sauté the onions on medium heat till brown. Drain well. Keep a few slices aside for garnishing.

❹ To the same oil, add the chopped garlic and sauté till light brown. Add the carrot and sauté for few minutes.

❺ Add the vegetable stock and bring it to a boil. Lower heat and let it simmer for ten to fifteen minutes.

❻ Add the salt and white pepper powder.

❼ To serve, ladle the soup into individual bowls, float the toasted brown bread, top it with grated cheese and fried brown onions and serve hot.

Chef's Tip: Since the quantity of oil used for frying the onion is minimal, the sliced onion would not become crisp as in the case of traditional French onion soup. However, if available, use dehydrated sliced onions, as they remain crisp.

Garlic acts as a rejuvenator. It removes toxins, revitalizes the blood and stimulates blood circulation. Carrots and cheese are rich in Vitamin A and calcium. So this soup is not just tasty it is very healthy too.

tomato
and basil soup

Ingredients

20-24 medium tomatoes, quartered
24 fresh basil leaves
2 bay leaves
20 black peppercorns
2 medium onions, sliced
8 garlic cloves, chopped
2 six-inch celery stalks, finely chopped
2 medium carrots, roughly chopped
Salt to taste
2 tablespoons gram flour
2 teaspoons sugar

Method

❶ Heat a non-stick pan. Add the bay leaves, half of the peppercorns and onions and roast until translucent.

❷ Add the garlic, celery and three tablespoons of water. Stir lightly.

❸ Add the carrots and tomatoes.

❹ Reserve six basil leaves for garnish and add the rest to the tomatoes.

❺ Stir and add salt. Cook on medium heat till the tomato pieces soften. Add three cups of water and bring it to a boil. Cover and cook for ten to fifteen minutes.

❻ Strain the mixture through a strainer. Reserve the liquid. Remove the peppercorns and bay leaves from the residue and allow it to cool. Blend in a mixer to get a smooth purée.

❼ Roast the gram flour in another pan till fragrant. Add the puréed tomatoes and mix.

❽ Add the reserved liquid and adjust the consistency. Return to the heat.

❾ Add the sugar, salt, freshly crushed remaining peppercorns and let it simmer for a couple of minutes. Strain and bring to a boil again.

❿ Garnish with the reserved basil leaves and serve piping hot.

Want a fresh glowing skin? Have tomatoes as they are rich in Vitamins A and C and the antioxidant lycopene. Basil, or *tulsi*, is rich in calcium, potassium, Vitamin A and is also low in fat.

mutton
pudina shorba

Ingredients

350 grams boneless lean mutton, cut
into ½-inch cubes
25-30 fresh mint leaves, roughly chopped
1 tablespoon olive oil/rice bran oil
1 teaspoon cumin seeds
1 medium onion, chopped
1 garlic clove, chopped
¼ teaspoon red chilli flakes
½ teaspoon cinnamon powder
1 green cardamom
2 medium tomatoes, skinned, seeded
and roughly chopped
½ cup chickpeas, boiled
A few saffron threads
Salt to taste
½ cup skimmed milk yogurt, whisked

Method

❶ Heat the oil in a pressure cooker; add the cumin seeds and sauté till they begin to change colour. Add the onion and sauté till translucent. Add the garlic, chilli flakes, mutton cubes and fresh mint. Continue to sauté for a few seconds.

❷ Add the cinnamon powder and cardamom and continue to sauté for two more minutes.

❸ Add the tomatoes, chickpeas, saffron, salt and six cups of water and bring to a boil. Pressure cook for around twenty-five minutes till the pressure is released six times (six whistles).

❹ Remove the lid when the pressure has reduced; add the yogurt and cook over low heat for two to three minutes. Serve hot.

Mutton is rich in protein and Vitamin B. This is an excellent soup for adolescent children who need extra proteins for growth and development. It can be given to nursing mothers too, as it is a galactagogue. Chickpeas add consistency as well as protein. Besides mint is a digestive aid.

about healthy foods

Let us look at the different types of foods and see how healthy they are. We will also see how small changes in a daily diet plan can help one eat healthier. We know food supplies us with various nutrients that play vital roles in keeping the body in good working order. For better understanding we can divide nutrients into Macro Nutrients and Micro Nutrients.

Macro Nutrients

• Carbohydrates

Simple carbohydrates: sugar, honey, jaggery.
Complex carbohydrates: roots and tubers, whole grains, cereals, *dals*, fruits and vegetables with seeds.

• Proteins

Animal origin: meat, fish, egg, poultry.
Plant origin: *dals*, pulses, nuts and oilseeds, milk and milk products.

• Fats

Visible fat: ghee, butter, oils, margarine.
Invisible fat: meat, nuts and oilseeds, milk and milk products.

Micro Nutrients

• Vitamins

Water-soluble vitamins: Vitamin B and Vitamin C.
Fat-soluble vitamins: Vitamin A, D, E, K.

• Minerals

Calcium, sodium, potassium, magnesium, iron, iodine, chromium, manganese, selenium, zinc and so on.

a look at fats

Fats store energy in a more concentrated form than carbohydrates. They are found in adipose tissue. It is recommended that no more than ten percent of your daily calorie intake should come from fat. Foods high in fat are generally high in calories and provide twice the calories of starch and protein. Cutting down on fatty foods is the fastest way to reduce your caloric intake. But it is important to include some fats in your diet as they are carriers for fat-soluble vitamins in the blood stream.

how do I maintain a healthy level of fats?

❶ Always check the label on a food product that mentions the amount of saturated fat in the particular food as 'sat fat' or 'saturates'. Cut down on processed foods, which are often heavy in saturated fats. If you want to munch on crisps, check the label and choose those with lower 'sat fat' as there is often a big difference between brands.

❷ Visualize the intake of fat in your diet and instead of pouring oil straight from the bottle into your food use a spray or measure out oil with a teaspoon.

❸ Avoid cooking with saturated fats such as butter and ghee. Replace with mono-unsaturated oils preferably olive oil, rice bran oil or groundnut oil or poly-unsaturated oils such as soyabean oil or sunflower oil.

❹ Choose low-fat varieties of dairy foods such as semi-skimmed, 1% fat milk or skimmed milk, low-fat yogurts and low-fat cheeses. Avoid full fat dairy products such as cream, *paneer* and yogurt. Try replacing *paneer* with tofu.

❺ Avoid using too much coconut in your cooking. Use low-fat coconut milk.

❻ Swap creamy sauces with tomato or vegetable-based options.

❼ Eat foods high in good fats, such as oily fish for omega-3, and limit foods that are high in dangerous saturated fat. Snack off a small handful of unsalted nuts instead of cakes, biscuits, *namkeen* and *mithai.*

a look at protein-rich foods

The primary function of proteins is to build new muscles and other tissues and repair old and worn-out ones. Sometimes intake of carbohydrates and fats is less because of which a person's daily requirement of these nutrients is not met. The body then starts drawing energy from proteins. This results in the loss of muscle mass and general weakening of the whole body.

The main advantage of a high-protein diet is that it triggers weight loss. Proteins have amino acids that promote good health. If your body is deficient in amino acids then you are bound to be unhealthy. If you follow a high-protein diet instead of a carbohydrate-rich one based on refined foods, then the body experiences a state of ketosis. It derives energy from burning fats when it does not find fuel in the form of carbohydrates. Thus consuming fewer carbohydrates means more burning of fats. Research has found that some sources of protein if consumed in a very oily and fried form can be harmful to your health rather than beneficial. Combining foods like grains and pulses or grains and milk products can provide complete proteins. The requirement of protein for every individual is different. A manual labourer, growing child, pregnant and lactating mother, and recuperating patient need a high-protein diet. A diet high in good-quality protein, which has all the essential amino acids, is achieved when two or three protein sources are combined together.

High protein	Moderate protein
Lean cuts of meat and poultry, fish, egg, dals, pulses, soyabean, tofu	Cereals and grains
Milk, paneer, nuts and oil seeds	

A person's daily requirement of protein is 1gm/kg of body weight, but ensure that good quality proteins are included.

a look at high-fibre foods

Fibre is classified as soluble and insoluble. The American Heart Association recommends that you eat at least 25-30 grams of dietary fibre, in both soluble and insoluble forms, every day. The ratio of calories to dietary fibre is the same: the more calories you consume to meet your daily needs the more dietary fibre you need to add in the diet. Try to eat at least 14 grams of fibre per 1,000 calories you consume. Fibre helps in the rapid removal of wastes from intestines. As a bonus, high-fibre foods are low in fat and high in vitamins and minerals. They are filling as well as satisfying and do not add much to your calorie count. Foods high in soluble fibre include oat bran, oatmeal, beans, peas, rice bran, barley, citrus fruits, strawberries and apple pulp. Foods high in insoluble fibre include wholewheat breads, wheat cereals, wheat bran, cabbage, beets, carrots, brussels sprouts, turnips, cauliflower and apple skin.

how do I add more fibre to my diet?

❶ Substitute low-fibre foods (white bread, white rice, candy and chips) with fibre-containing foods (whole-grain bread, brown rice, fruits and vegetables).

❷ Try to eat more raw vegetables and fresh fruit, including the skins when suitable. Cooking vegetables can reduce their fibre content, and skins are a good source of fibre.

❸ Eat high-fibre foods at every meal. Bran cereal for breakfast is a good start, but try to include some fruits, vegetables, whole-grains and beans in your diet, too.

❹ Be sure to increase your fibre intake gradually, giving your body time to adjust, and drink at least eight to ten 200 ml glasses of water a day.

a look at iron-rich foods

Iron is necessary for many functions in the body including formation of haemoglobin, brain development and function, regulation of body temperature, and for muscle activity. Iron is essential for binding oxygen to the blood cells. The first symptoms of iron deficiency are fatigue, weakness, rapid heartbeat, fainting spells, susceptibility to infection, and swelling of the tongue.

how do I improve my intake of iron?

❶ Include daily physical activity such as brisk walking. Regular, steady activity encourages the marrow to produce more blood cells.

❷ Minimize smoking, since smoking restricts the oxygen-carrying capacity of the blood.

❸ Eat meat, poultry or fish at the same time as green vegetables or beans. This is because the meat, besides containing iron, helps absorb iron from other foods that contain iron, when had at the same time.

❹ Include fruit and vegetables that are high in Vitamin C as part of your meals. Try a glass of orange juice with breakfast, a tomato salad at lunchtime and a piece of fruit with your evening meal. This is because Vitamin C helps you absorb iron from food.

❺ Do not drink tea at mealtimes or for half an hour afterwards. This is because the tannin in tea reduces the amount of iron absorbed from food.

❻ Use iron vessels for cooking vegetables and *dals*.

some iron-rich foods

Prune juice, liver, black beans, *moong*, baked beans, garden cress seeds, soybeans, rice bran, turkey, rice, lentils, spinach, dry peaches, shrimps, raw oysters, split peas, peas, beet greens, black-eyed peas, chocolate, raisins, dates, tofu, tomato juice, pumpkin seeds, wheat bran, wheat germ, soybean milk, dry figs, broccoli, strawberries, potatoes, oatmeal, eggs and mushrooms.

a look at calcium-rich foods

Your bones and teeth contain about 99% of the calcium in your body! Calcium is so important that if you do not eat enough of calcium-rich foods, the body will suck the calcium from your bones to maintain the calcium levels in the blood. If this carries on, your bones will no longer be strong. It is very important to take in enough calcium to keep your bones healthy and strong!

how do I maintain my calcium stores?

❶ Adequate calcium and vitamin D intake (recommendations differ from country to country, varying between 800 to 1300 mg per day, depending on age).

❷ Avoid under-nutrition and protein malnutrition.

❸ Maintain an adequate supply of Vitamin D through sufficient exposure to the sun and through diet.

❹ Participate in regular physical activity.

❺ Avoid smoking.

❻ Do weight-bearing exercises regularly.

❼ Avoid heavy drinking.

❽ Persons of middle age and beyond should follow these fundamental principles. They should also assess their risk of developing osteoporosis and, with medical advice, consider medications to help maintain an optimal bone mass and to decrease the risk of fracture.

food sources

Vitamin C helps maintain collagen that helps strengthen teeth and bones. One good source is tomato. Leafy greens have the highest amount of calcium. Coriander, fenugreek and spinach all have enough calcium, which is absorbed into the blood very easily. Broccoli is another vegetable that is a good source of calcium. Yogurt has plenty of calcium and makes a great end to your meals. Healthy alternatives for mid-morning snacks are prunes and oranges, which are great sources. Green peas can be added to almost all foods. Do not get misled by their size: they pack a large amount of calcium. Soya is a good source of calcium, which makes a good alternative for those who are lactose-intolerant.

snacks &
starters

pan-fried mushrooms

Ingredients

20-24 fresh button mushrooms, quartered
½ cup porcini mushrooms (optional)
½ cup oyster mushrooms (optional)
1 small red capsicum, seeded and cut into
½-inch pieces
1 small yellow capsicum, seeded and cut
into ½-inch pieces
1 tablespoon olive oil
2 medium onions, cut into ½-inch cubes
3 garlic cloves, crushed
1 tablespoon soy sauce
1 tablespoon red chilli sauce
½ tablespoon vinegar
½ teaspoon dried thyme
Salt to taste
8-10 black peppercorns, crushed
7-8 fresh basil leaves, torn

Method

❶ If using porcini and oyster mushrooms, soak them in lukewarm water for twenty minutes. Drain. Wash well and set aside.

❷ Heat the oil in a large non-stick pan. Add the onions and sauté over medium heat. When they turn translucent, add the garlic and stir-fry for a minute.

❸ Add the mushrooms and the red and yellow capsicums and sauté on high heat for three minutes.

❹ Add the soy sauce, chilli sauce and vinegar and sauté for a further two minutes.

❺ Add the thyme, salt and crushed peppercorns.

❻ Remove from heat, stir in the basil leaves and serve hot.

This is an exciting stir-fry for mushroom-lovers. The vegetables and mushrooms remain crunchy and the capsicums provide Vitamin C.

quesadillas

Ingredients

Tortillas
1 cup cornmeal
½ cup wholewheat flour
Salt to taste
¼ cup milk

Filling
6 teaspoons olive oil
2 medium onions, chopped
6-8 garlic cloves, chopped
2 cups kidney beans, boiled
6 tablespoons tomato ketchup
4 green chillies, chopped
2 teaspoons paprika
Salt to taste
2 cups grated cheese
4 tablespoons chopped fresh coriander

Method

❶ Mix together the cornmeal, wholewheat flour and salt. Knead into a soft dough with milk and half a cup of water. Cover with a damp piece of muslin and set aside for a few minutes.

❷ Divide the dough into eight equal portions and roll each portion into a thin ten-inch round tortilla (*chapati*). Lightly cook each tortilla on a hot *tawa* on both sides and set aside.

❸ To make the filling, heat two teaspoons of oil in a pan and sauté the onions and garlic for one minute.

❹ Add the boiled kidney beans, tomato ketchup, green chillies, paprika and salt and cook for two to three minutes.

❺ Heat a *tawa* and place a tortilla on it. Spread one-fourth portion of the filling, top with one-fourth portion of the cheese and fresh coriander. Cover with another tortilla.

❻ Drizzle one teaspoon oil all around. Turn the tortilla over gently when the underside is cooked. Cook the other side. Similarly make three more quesadillas with the remaining ingredients.

❼ Remove, cut into wedges and serve hot.

A touch of easy Mexican for your daily menu. Another plus point: it's really nutritious.

dilli aloo kachalu chaat

Ingredients

2 large potatoes, parboiled and cut into 1-inch pieces
1 large sweet potato, parboiled and cut into 1-inch pieces
2 teaspoons lemon juice
Salt to taste
1 inch ginger, cut into thin strips
2 tablespoons oil
1 tablespoon Date and Tamarind Chutney (Vol. 5, page 65)
1 teaspoon *chaat masala*
½ teaspoon red chilli powder
2 teaspoons roasted cumin powder
2 green chillies, chopped
3 tablespoons chopped fresh coriander

Method

❶ In a small bowl, add one teaspoon lemon juice and a pinch of salt to the ginger strips and keep in the refrigerator till use.

❷ Heat the oil in a non-stick pan till medium hot. Place the potato pieces and sauté till crisp and golden. Drain on absorbent paper.

❸ Add the sweet potato pieces to the same oil and sauté till crisp and golden. Drain on absorbent paper.

❹ Transfer the potatoes and sweet potatoes into a big bowl. Add the salt, date and tamarind chutney, *chaat masala*, chilli powder, cumin powder, green chilies, fresh coriander and the remaining lemon juice and mix well.

❺ To serve, transfer the mixture into a serving bowl, garnish with ginger strips and serve immediately.

Potatoes and sweet potatoes are a good source of energy and complex carbohydrates, which keep you full for a longer time.

green chana chaat

Ingredients

1½ cups dried green Bengal gram, soaked overnight
2 medium onions, chopped
2 medium tomatoes, chopped
2-3 green chillies, chopped
2 tablespoons chopped fresh coriander
Black salt to taste
1 teaspoon roasted cumin powder
1 teaspoon *chaat masala*
½ teaspoon red chilli powder
2 tablespoons lemon juice

Method

❶ Pressure cook the soaked green *chana* in three cups of water till the pressure is released two to three times (two to three whistles) or till done.

❷ Transfer the *chana* into a *kadai* and simmer till all the water evaporates.

❸ Place the hot *chana* in a bowl. Add the onions, tomatoes, green chillies, fresh coriander, black salt, roasted cumin powder, *chaat masala*, chilli powder and lemon juice and mix well.

❹ Serve immediately.

Though best made with fresh green *chana* in season, you can use dried ones too. Perk them up with spring onion greens and chopped *paneer* or tofu. Colour and taste attract children since these two factors increase the palatability of the dish.

fruit chaat

Ingredients

½ small papaya, cut into 1-inch cubes
2 kiwi fruits, cut into 1-inch cubes
½ cup pomegranate kernels
½ cup orange segments
½ cup sweet lime segments
1 medium apple, cut into 1-inch cubes
¼ cup seedless green grapes, halved
¼ cup seedless black grapes, halved
½ teaspoon red chilli powder
1½ tablespoons *chaat masala*
Rock salt to taste
1 tablespoon lemon juice

Method

❶ Place the papaya, kiwi fruits, pomegranate, orange and sweet lime segments, apple and green and black grapes in a large bowl and place in a refrigerator to chill thoroughly.

❷ Just before serving, sprinkle chilli powder, *chaat masala* and rock salt. Add the lemon juice and toss the fruits well. Serve immediately.

Fruits all put together make a splendid sight indeed. Try adding a few fresh mint leaves for those little bursts of freshness. Fruits are an excellent snack to have in-between meals. In fact this medley can be made with any seasonal fruits.

peanut chaat

Ingredients

2 cups raw peanuts in their shells
1 tablespoon sea salt
1 teaspoon turmeric powder
Salt to taste
¼ teaspoon *chaat masala*
½ teaspoon red chilli powder
1 teaspoon roasted cumin powder
1 medium onion, chopped
1 medium tomato, chopped
2 green chillies, chopped
2 tablespoons chopped fresh coriander
2 tablespoons lemon juice

Method

❶ Pressure-cook the peanuts in five cups of water with sea salt and turmeric powder till the pressure is released four to five times (four to five whistles).

❷ Drain and shell the peanuts.

❸ Place the peanuts in a bowl. Add the salt, chaat masala, chilli powder, roasted cumin powder, onion, tomato, green chillies, fresh coriander, lemon juice and mix well.

❹ Serve hot or cold.

This recipe is a contribution from Alyona, whose friend had served it at a kitty party. The only time-consuming part is the shelling of the peanuts, otherwise it is a quick recipe.

rajma galouti kababs

Ingredients

1 cup red kidney beans
8 cashew nuts
1 tablespoon *chironji*
½ teaspoon caraway seeds
4 green cardamoms
3 black cardamoms
2 cloves
½ inch cinnamon
A generous pinch of saffron
¼ teaspoon *kewra* water
1 tablespoon oil + for greasing the pan
½ inch ginger, chopped
5 garlic cloves, chopped
3 green chillies, chopped
2 tablespoons grated *khoya/mawa*
½ teaspoon white pepper powder
Salt to taste
½ tablespoon lemon juice
1 sprig fresh mint 1 medium onion,
cut into thin rings

Method

❶ Soak the *rajma* in plenty of water overnight. Drain and boil in plenty of fresh water until the beans are tender. Drain and set aside.

❷ Dry-roast the cashew nuts and *chironji* and grind together using a little water to a fine paste.

❸ Dry-roast the caraway seeds, green and black cardamoms, cloves and cinnamon. Cool and grind to a fine powder.

❹ Soak the saffron in the *kewra* water.

❺ Heat the oil in a non-stick pan, add the ginger and garlic and sauté for a few seconds. Add the chillies and sauté for one minute.

❻ Add the boiled *rajma* and cook for three to four minutes. Add the cashew nut paste and stir-fry for four to five minutes. Add the *khoya*, white pepper powder and salt. Stir-fry for another four to five minutes. Remove the pan from the heat and leave the beans to cool.

❼ Mash the *rajma* to a smooth paste. (If the paste is not firm, cook it further in a non-stick pan to thicken it). Sprinkle the roasted spice powder and soaked saffron.

❽ Mix in the lemon juice, divide the mixture into eight equal portions. Press them lightly into *tikki*.

❾ Heat a non-stick pan and grease it lightly. Cook the *tikki* until lightly coloured on both sides. Serve hot, garnished with the mint and onion rings.

The vegetarian version of the famous, melt-in the-mouth lamb *galouti kabab* can be made variously with yam, peas or spinach, but the ones using red kidney beans come closest to the original delicacy. Kidney beans are a very good source of cholesterol-lowering fibre, as are most other beans. In addition their high-fibre content prevents blood sugar levels from rising too rapidly after a meal, making these beans an especially good choice for individuals with diabetes, insulin resistance or hypoglycemia.

hara bhara kabab

Ingredients

100 grams fresh spinach leaves,
blanched and chopped
¾ cup shelled green peas, boiled and mashed
3-4 medium potatoes, boiled and grated
2 green chillies, chopped
2 tablespoons chopped fresh coriander
1 inch ginger, chopped
1 teaspoon *chaat masala*
Salt to taste
2 tablespoons cornflour
2 tablespoons olive oil

Method

❶ Mix together the spinach, peas and potatoes. Add the green chillies, fresh coriander, ginger, *chaat masala* and salt. Add the cornflour for binding.

❷ Divide the mixture into twenty-four portions. Shape each portion into a ball and then press it between your palms to give it a flat *tikki* shape.

❸ Heat the oil in a non-stick pan. Shallow-fry the *tikki* for two to three minutes on each side.

❹ Drain on absorbent paper and serve hot.

Hara Bhara Kabab is one of my favourite recipes. I would recommend that you do not add artificial colour to this recipe. You may increase the quantity of spinach leaves for a darker green colour. In that case add a little more cornflour for binding.

masala dosa chaat

Ingredients

2 cups *dosa* batter
Red Chilli-Garlic Chutney (Vol. 4, page 68),
as required
1½ cups potato *bhaji,* lightly mashed
2 large onions, chopped
2 large tomatoes, chopped
1 teaspoon red chilli powder
1½ teaspoons *chaat masala*
Oil for shallow-frying
2 tablespoons chopped fresh coriander

Ragda
½ cup dried white peas, soaked overnight
¼ teaspoon turmeric powder
A pinch of asafoetida
Salt to taste
2 teaspoons *chaat masala*
2 teaspoons Date and Tamarind Chutney
(Vol. 5, page 65)

Method

❶ For the *ragda*, pressure cook the dried white peas in three cups of water with the turmeric powder, asafoetida and salt till the pressure is released four to five times (four to five whistles) or till soft. Mash the peas slightly. Add the *chaat masala* and date and tamarind chutney and a little water if too thick and simmer for ten minutes. Keep the *ragda* hot.

❷ Heat and season a non-stick *dosa tawa.* Place a small ladleful of *dosa* bat ter on the *tawa* and spread evenly to make an eight-inch diameter *dosa*. Drizzle half a teaspoon of oil around the *dosa* and cook on low heat for half a minute.

❸ Spread a little red chilli-garlic chutney all over the *dosa*. Sprinkle some onions, tomatoes, chilli powder and *chaat masala*. Place a small portion of potato *bhaji in the centre*. Press gently with a back of a ladle till lightly mashed and spread all over the *dosa*. Drizzle some more oil and cook over low heat so that the underside turns golden and crisp.

❹ Roll the *dosa* up tightly like a spring roll, transfer onto a plate and cut into equal lengths Similarly arrange on a serving platter.

❺ Spoon *ragda* generously over the *dosa,* garnish with fresh coriander and serve hot.

Accept the compliments that come your way for this creative presentation! Ensure that the *radga* is warm. Don't skip the red chilli-garlic chutney because that is what adds the maximum punch.

dabeli

Ingredients

4 round buns
1½ tablespoons *dabeli masala* powder
2 tablespoons olive oil/rice bran oil
2 large potatoes, boiled and mashed
Salt to taste
1 teaspoon lemon juice
1 cup Date and Tamarind Chutney (Vol. 5, page 65)
1 tablespoon sugar
½ cup *masala moongphali*
¼ cup grated coconut
¼ cup fresh pomegranate kernels
10-12 black grapes, chopped
½ cup nylon sev
2 tablespoons chopped fresh coriander
¼ cup Red Chilli-Garlic Chutney (Vol. 4, page 68)
2 medium onions, chopped

Method

❶ Heat one tablespoon oil in a non-stick pan. Add the potatoes, salt and a little water. Mix well and add the *dabeli masala*, lemon juice, half a cup of date and tamarind chutney and sugar. Mix and cook till the moisture is absorbed. Spread the mixture on a plate.

❷ Sprinkle the *masala* peanuts, coconut, pomegranate, black grapes, half the *sev* and fresh coriander over the top.

❸ Slit the *pavs* horizontally without cutting through. Spread the red chilli-garlic chutney, a layer of the potato stuffing, date and tamarind chutney, onion and *sev* in between the two halves.

❹ Place the stuffed *pav* on a hot nonstick *tawa*. Press slightly and toast on both sides with the remaining oil till done. Serve immediately.

There is something about this sandwich that makes it so endearing: that something is the *masala* perhaps, or the crunch of the peanuts, or the punch of the chutneys... ask any kid what they want to eat and very often the answer will be '*Dabeli*'! This popular street snack can be made using less oil and butter at home.

masala khichia papad

ngredients

8 *khichia papad*
8 teaspoons butter
4 tablespoons Green Chutney (Vol. 4, page 72)
2 tablespoons Red Chilli-Garlic Chutney
(Vol. 4, page 68)
2 tablespoons *chaat masala*
4-5 tablespoons chopped fresh coriander

Method

❶ Dry-roast all the *khichia papad* till crisp.

❷ Drizzle one teaspoon of butter over each *papad*, and top with dollops of the chutneys.

❸ Sprinkle *chaat masala* and fresh coriander and serve immediately before the *papad* becomes soggy.

This is something exclusive as it is a roadside treat in the western parts of the country. It is a simple *papad* made glorious with chutneys... something that can be rustled up at home at a moment's notice. Marwaris make their own *khichia* and usually serve it as a snack; roasted crisp with blackened edges and drizzled quite liberally with pure ghee and chilli powder.

vegetable seekh kabab

Ingredients

1 medium potato, boiled and mashed
1 medium carrot, grated
½ cup green peas, crushed
5-6 French beans, finely chopped
1 teaspoon ginger paste
1 teaspoon dried mango powder
2 teaspoons *chaat masala*
3-4 green chillies, chopped
1½ tablespoons *chhunda*
3 tablespoons roasted Bengal gram powder
150 grams skimmed milk cottage cheese, grated
Salt to taste

Method

❶ Heat a non-stick *kadai*. Add the ginger paste and cook for half a minute. Add the mashed potato, carrot, green peas and French beans and roast till fragrant.

❷ Add the dried mango powder, *chaat masala*, green chillies, *chhunda* and the roasted Bengal gram powder and continue to cook for two to three minutes.

❸ Add the cottage cheese and mix well. Add the salt and mix again.

❹ Divide into eight equal portions. Take each portion and mould it around a skewer in a cylindrical shape.

❺ Heat a non-stick *tawa* and place the skewers on it. Cook on medium heat, rotating the skewers from time to time so that the *kababs* get cooked evenly from all sides, to a golden brown.

❻ Serve hot with a chutney of your choice.

Why not serve these at your next party? Simple to make, they look great and will encourage your friends to go in for low-fat cooking! Filled with veggies, these *kababs* are good for health.

fish tikka achaari

Ingredients

2 (400 grams) *surmai* fillets,
cut into 2-inch pieces
2 tablespoons lemon juice
Salt to taste
1 teaspoon garlic paste
1 teaspoon ginger paste
½ teaspoon turmeric powder
2 teaspoons Kashmiri red chilli powder
1 teaspoon mustard seeds, roasted
1 teaspoon fennel seeds
1 teaspoon onion seeds
½ teaspoon fenugreek seeds
½ teaspoon black salt
1 tablespoon mustard oil
1 cup skimmed milk yogurt, whisked
2 tablespoons butter, melted

Method

❶ Place the fish in a bowl; add the lemon juice, salt, garlic paste, ginger paste, turmeric powder and chilli powder and mix.

❷ Heat a pan and dry-roast the mustard seeds, fennel seeds, onion seeds and fenugreek seeds. Crush them with black salt in a mortar with a pestle.

❸ Heat the mustard oil in a pan to smoking point. Set aside to cool.

❹ Add the yogurt to the fish along with the crushed spices and mix. Let it stand for thirty minutes.

❺ Preheat an oven to 200°C/400°F/Gas Mark 6.

❻ When the mustard oil cools completely add it to the marinated fish and mix.

❼ Place the fish on a greased rack and place the rack in the preheated oven with a tray underneath it and cook.

❽ Baste once with butter and cook for ten to fifteen minutes or till done.

❾ Serve hot.

Chef's Tip: If you do not have an oven, you can skewer the pieces on satay sticks and cook them on a non-stick *tawa*.

Don't be surprised at the rate at which these are polished off the platter! As fish absorbs flavours well, the pickling spices and mustard oil make this a truly spectacular starter. Fenugreek seeds are rich in iron and calcium and help reduce cholesterol and blood sugar levels.

broken wheat upma

Ingredients

1 cup fine broken wheat
¼ cup skimmed milk yogurt
Salt to taste
¼ teaspoon mustard seeds
1 teaspoon split black gram
10-12 curry leaves
1 medium onion, chopped
1 inch ginger, chopped
3-4 green chillies, chopped
1 medium carrot, diced and blanched
¼ cup green peas, blanched
1 teaspoon lemon juice
2 tablespoons chopped fresh coriander

Method

❶ Whisk the yogurt, salt and three-and-a-half cups of water in a bowl till smooth. Set aside.

❷ Heat a non-stick pan. Add the mustard seeds and split black gram. When the mustard seeds splutter, add the curry leaves and onion, and cook till lightly browned.

❸ Stir in the broken wheat and continue to cook on medium heat for two minutes. Add the ginger and chillies and cook for another five minutes, or until fragrant.

❹ Mix in the yogurt mixture and bring to a boil. Cook the *upma* on low heat, stirring continuously, until all the water is absorbed.

❺ Add the carrot and peas, along with the lemon juice. Stir gently, adjust the seasoning, and add a little more water if required.

❻ Cover and cook on low heat for another eight to ten minutes.

❼ Transfer into a serving bowl, garnish with fresh coriander and serve hot.

Upma is a wholesome dish made traditionally with semolina, but some regions use cracked wheat. I cannot make my mind up about this dish… should I eat it for breakfast or as a light meal? It tastes so good! You can use a pressure cooker for the recipe, but I prefer this slow-cooking method as the wheat swells up more, making it tastier. You could use broccoli instead of carrot and blanched sweetcorn instead of peas – experiment with your favourite combinations of vegetables.

makai, badam aur akhrot ki tikki

Ingredients

1½ cups corn kernels, boiled and ground
20 almonds, blanched, peeled and ground
16 walnut halves, chopped
200 grams lotus roots
3 tablespoons olive oil/rice bran oil
1 teaspoon caraway seeds
1 teaspoon red chilli powder
1 teaspoon black pepper powder
1 teaspoon fennel powder
1 teaspoon *garam masala* powder
1 teaspoon *chaat masala*
100 grams skimmed milk cottage cheese, grated
Salt to taste
¼ cup grated low-fat processed cheese
1 tablespoon lemon juice
1 inch ginger, chopped
2 tablespoons chopped fresh coriander
24 raisins, chopped

Method

❶ Clean and scrape the lotus roots. Grate and boil until soft. Drain and squeeze out excess water. Grind to a paste. Set aside.

❷ Heat one tablespoon oil in a non-stick *kadai*, add the caraway seeds and sauté till fragrant. Add the corn, almond and lotus root pastes and sauté till the mixture dries up.

❸ Add the chilli powder, pepper powder, fennel powder, *garam masala* powder and *chaat masala* and mix well. Add the *paneer* and salt and mix well. Cook till the mixture thickens and leaves the sides of the *kadai*.

❹ Remove from heat and add the processed cheese, lemon juice, ginger and fresh coriander. Set aside to cool.

❺ Divide the cooled mixture into twenty equal balls. Stuff the balls with walnuts and raisins and shape them into *tikkis*.

❻ Shallow-fry the *tikkis* on a non-stick frying pan using the remaining oil, in two batches. Drain on absorbent paper.

❼ Serve hot with Green Chutney (Vol. 4, page 72)

Does the list of ingredients in this recipe seem long? Marvel at it because the intermingling of all the flavours and textures makes this *tikki* recipe unsurpassed. With all the nuts and raisins, the *tikki* is rich in anti-oxidants and hence a wonderful energy-giving snack.

patra

Ingredients

12 colocasia leaves
1½ cups gram flour
2 teaspoons coriander powder
2 teaspoons roasted cumin powder
1 teaspoon red chilli powder
1 teaspoon turmeric powder
2 teaspoons sesame seeds
½ teaspoon soda bicarbonate
Salt to taste
2 teaspoons green chilli paste
2 teaspoons ginger paste
2 tablespoons oil
¼ teaspoon *garam masala* powder
3½ tablespoons grated jaggery
1 lemon-sized ball of tamarind
1 teaspoon mustard seeds
A pinch of asafoetida
2 tablespoons grated fresh coconut
2 tablespoons chopped fresh coriander

Method

❶ Remove the thick stem from the leaves. Wash the leaves, wipe dry and set aside.

❷ To make the *masala*, mix together the gram flour, coriander powder, roasted cumin powder, chilli powder and turmeric powder in a bowl. Add the sesame seeds, soda bicarbonate, salt, green chilli paste, ginger paste, one tablespoon oil, *garam masala* powder and jaggery. Mix well.

❸ Soak the tamarind in a cup of water. Strain the water. Mix in the juice with the gram flour mixture to form a paste.

❹ Place a leaf, shiny side face down on a work surface. Spread the *masala* evenly over the back of the leaf. Place another leaf over it, but with its tapering end in the opposite direction of the first one. Spread some paste over it. Similarly use up three leaves per roll.

❺ Fold in the four edges and gently roll into a tight cylinder. Tie it up with a string. Do the same with the rest of the leaves and paste.

❻ Steam the rolls in a steamer for about fifteen to twenty minutes, or till cooked. Remove and set aside to cool. Cut into one-and-a half-inch thick pieces.

❼ Heat the remaining oil in a non-stick pan. Add the mustard seeds. When they begin to crackle, add the asafoetida and the slices of *patra*. Sauté till golden brown.

❽ Serve hot, garnished with the fresh coconut and coriander.

Patra recipes vary from home to home and region to region. The best ones I have had are those made by my mum-in-law.

pav bhaji roll-ups

Ingredients

4 tortilla wraps
8 lettuce leaves

Pav bhaji
1 tablespoon oil
2 medium onions, chopped
3-4 green chillies, chopped
2 teaspoons ginger paste
2 teaspoons garlic paste
4 medium tomatoes, chopped
1 medium green capsicum, seeded and chopped
¼ cup green peas, boiled and mashed lightly
¼ small cauliflower, grated
4 medium potatoes, boiled and grated
1½ tablespoons *pav bhaji masala*
Salt to taste
2 tablespoons chopped fresh coriander

Onion-cheese mixture
1 large onion, sliced
2 large tomatoes, seeded and sliced
½ cup grated processed cheese
½ teaspoon red chilli powder

Method

❶ To make the *pav bhaji*, heat the oil in a non-stick pan and add three-fourth of the onions. Sauté on medium heat till light brown. Add the green chillies, ginger paste and garlic paste. Sauté for half a minute.

❷ Add half the tomatoes and cook on medium heat for three to four minutes, stirring continuously or till the oil separates from the *masala*.

❸ Add the green capsicum, green peas, cauliflower, potatoes and one-and-a-half cups of water. Bring it to a boil and simmer for ten minutes, pressing with the back of the spoon a few times, till all the vegetables are completely mashed.

❹ Add the *pav bhaji masala*, salt and the remaining tomatoes. Cook on medium heat for two minutes, stirring continuously.

❺ Place the *bhaji* in a *kadai* and simmer for five to ten minutes, stirring often, till all the moisture evaporates and the *bhaji* is dry. Add the fresh coriander and mix. Transfer to a bowl and set aside.

❻ Combine the ingredients for the onion-cheese mixture in a bowl and set aside.

❼ Heat a *tawa* and lightly warm the tortillas on both the sides.

❽ Place a warmed tortilla on a square piece of aluminium foil. Spread one-fourth of the *bhaji* over the tortilla and generously sprinkle a fourth of the onion-cheese mixture over it.

❾ Place two lettuce leaves on one side of the roll and roll it up tightly.

❿ Fold in the foil and serve. Make the remaining roll-ups in the similar way.

Pav bhaji is a popular street food in Mumbai. Make a variation with tortillas instead of bread. *Pav bhaji* is best enjoyed fresh and straight off the stove.

corn bhel

Ingredients

1 cup corn kernels
1 large onion, finely chopped
1 large tomato, finely chopped
2 medium potatoes, boiled and cut into ½-inch cubes
2 teaspoons *chaat masala* powder
3-4 green chillies, chopped
2 tablespoons Green Chutney (Vol. 4, page 72)
2 tablespoons Date and Tamarind Chutney (Vol. 5, page 65)
4 tablespoons fresh coriander, finely chopped
1½ teaspoons lemon juice
Salt to taste
1 cup cornflakes, crushed

Method

❶ Bring three cups of water to a boil. Add the corn kernels and continue to boil for three to four minutes. Drain. This *bhel* can be made with hot or cold corn kernels.

❷ Mix together the corn kernels, onion, tomato, potatoes, *chaat masala*, chillies, chutneys and fresh coriander. Add the lemon juice and salt and mix.

❸ Divide into individual servings, sprinkle the cornflakes and serve immediately.

I love this snack and enjoy it more during the rainy season. Sweetcorn is popular roasted on the cob but this refined version is so good that you can have it often! This *bhel* will come as a relief for mothers of growing children... this is an excellent snack for the hungry hordes. It is energy-giving and high in protein.

saunfia paneer tikka

Ingredients

500 grams skimmed milk cottage cheese
½ teaspoon Lucknowi fennel powder
2 tablespoons gram flour
¼ teaspoon turmeric powder
½ tablespoon ginger paste
½ tablespoon garlic paste
½ teaspoon white pepper powder
Salt to taste
2 tablespoons lemon juice
½ teaspoon green cardamom powder
A few saffron threads
1 cup drained skimmed milk yogurt
2 medium green capsicums, seeded and
cut into 1½-inch squares
1½ teaspoons *chaat masala*

Method

❶ Cut the cottage cheese or *paneer* into
one-and-a-half-inch squares of half-inch
thickness.

❷ Heat a non-stick pan. Add the gram flour
and roast on medium heat until fragrant.
Remove from heat and add the turmeric
powder and mix. Cool and transfer to a bowl.

❸ Add the ginger paste, garlic paste, white
pepper powder, salt, one tablespoon of lemon
juice, cardamom powder, fennel powder, saf
fron and yogurt, mix and prepare a batter.

❹ Add the *paneer* cubes to the batter and
marinate for at least an hour.

❺ Thread the *paneer* cubes and the capsicum
squares alternately onto the skewers.

❻ Roast in a *tandoor*/charcoal grill for five
minutes till the *tikki* are golden in colour.

❼ Alternatively you can cook the *tikki* in
a convection oven or on a grill. Preheat an
oven to 220°C/425°F/Gas Mark 7 and cook for
three minutes on either side.

❽ Remove and sprinkle with the *chaat masala*
and the remaining lemon juice. Serve with
a chutney of your choice.

Paneer would probably be the one food that
is the children's favourite! But when you
are at your wit's end searching for different
recipes, try this one flavoured superbly with
saunf. Paneer requires careful handling while
cooking and is best not over-cooked.

teriyaki rolls

Ingredients

4 medium crusty rolls
1 tablespoon olive oil
2 medium green capsicums, seeded and sliced
10 medium fresh button mushrooms, sliced
1 large onion, sliced
½ cup firm tofu cubes

Sauce
1 tablespoon butter
1 inch ginger, sliced
1 medium onion, finely chopped
½ cup white wine
12-15 black grapes, crushed
1 tablespoon soy sauce
½ teaspoon black pepper powder
Salt to taste
1 tablespoon molasses
2 tablespoons honey

Method

❶ To make the teriyaki sauce, heat the butter in a non-stick pan. Add the ginger and onion and sauté till golden.

❷ Add the white wine and cook till the mixture reduces a little.

❸ Add the crushed black grapes and continue to cook, stirring for five to seven minutes till the grapes become soft.

❹ Add the soy sauce, black pepper powder, salt, molasses and honey. Mix well and strain the sauce. Set it aside.

❺ Heat the oil in a pan, add the capsicum, mushrooms, onion and tofu and toss for two minutes.

❻ Add the teriyaki sauce and mix. Cook for two minutes. Divide the mixture into four portions.

❼ Halve the crusty rolls and spread one portion of the vegetable and tofu mixture on one half of each roll and cover it with the other half.

❽ Serve immediately.

A taste of Japanese splendour, in a handy tofu-filled roll. Tofu is an excellent source of protein.

paneer tikka kali mirch

Ingredients

12-15 black peppercorns
500 grams skimmed milk cottage cheese,
cut into 1-inch cubes
1 inch ginger
6-8 garlic cloves
2-3 green chillies
1 tablespoon rice bran oil
4 medium onions, sliced
1 cup drained skimmed milk yogurt
1½ tablespoons fresh low-fat cream
1 tablespoon cornflour
1 egg white
½ teaspoon garam masala powder
1 medium green capsicum, seeded and
cut into 1-inch pieces
Salt to taste
¼ teaspoon green cardamom powder
1 tablespoon butter, for basting

Method

❶ Dry-roast the black peppercorns and crush to a coarse powder. Grind the ginger, garlic and green chillies to a fine paste.

❷ Heat the oil in a non-stick *kadai* and sauté the onions till brown. Cool and grind to a paste.

❸ In a large bowl, combine the browned onion paste, drained yogurt, fresh cream, cornflour, egg white, ginger-garlic-green chilli paste, *garam masala* powder, green capsicum pieces, crushed black peppercorns, salt and green cardamom powder. Add the *paneer* cubes, mix well and set aside to marinate for one hour, preferably in a refrigerator.

❹ Arrange the *paneer* cubes and capsicum cubes alternately on a skewer and grill for five to six minutes basting occasionally with butter.

❺ Serve hot with onion rings and Mint Chutney (Vol. 5, page 65).

Paneer and pepper have always been a friendly twosome. *Paneer* is a favourite food of most kids and it is healthy for them as they are active and need the calories.

tandoori murgh chaat

Ingredients

2 boneless chicken breasts, skin removed
1 teaspoon Kashmiri red chilli powder
1 teaspoon ginger paste
1 teaspoon garlic paste
½ cup drained skimmed milk yogurt
Salt to taste
1 tablespoon lemon juice
½ teaspoon *garam masala* powder
1½ tablespoons olive oil
1 small green capsicum, seeded and cut into thin strips
½ small red capsicum, seeded and cut into thin strips
½ small yellow capsicum, seeded and cut into thin strips
1 medium onion, sliced
2 green chillies, chopped
2 tablespoons chopped fresh coriander
1 tablespoon lemon juice
1 teaspoon *chaat masala*
½ small unripe green mango, chopped (optional)

Method

❶ Make incisions with a sharp knife on the chicken breasts and set aside.

❷ Combine together the chilli powder, ginger paste, garlic paste, drained yogurt, salt, lemon juice, *garam masala* powder and two teaspoons oil. Rub the mixture on the chicken and marinate for three to four hours preferably in a refrigerator.

❸ Preheat an oven to 200°C/400°F/Gas Mark 6.

❹ Thread the chicken onto skewers and cook in the preheated oven or in a moderately hot *tandoor* for ten to twelve minutes or until almost done. Baste with the remaining oil and cook for another four minutes. When cold, shred the chicken and set aside.

❺ In a large bowl, combine together the shredded chicken, green, red and yellow capsicum strips, onion, green chillies, half the fresh coriander, lemon juice, *chaat masala*, unripe green mango (if using) and salt and toss to mix well.

❻ Transfer onto a serving plate and serve garnished with the remaining fresh coriander.

There are three words that Indians are fond of: *tandoori, murgh* and *chaat*! This salad is the perfect fusion of all three.

paneer ke tinke

Ingredients

300 grams cottage cheese, cut into 1-inch
pieces
3 teaspoons oil
2 tablespoons gram flour
¾ cup drained skimmed milk yogurt
1 teaspoon roasted cumin powder
3-4 black peppercorns, crushed
½ teaspoon roasted and crushed dried
fenugreek leaves
½ teaspoon turmeric powder
½ teaspoon *garam masala* powder
5 teaspoons lemon juice
Salt to taste
A few saffron threads (optional)
1 medium onion, cut into 1-inch pieces and
layers separated
1 medium green capsicum, seeded and
cut into 1-inch pieces
1 medium red capsicum, seeded and
cut into 1-inch pieces

To serve
Mint Chutney (Vol. 5, page 65) as required

Method

❶ Heat one teaspoon oil in a pan and roast
the gram flour on low heat till fragrant.

❷ Place the drained yogurt, cumin powder,
peppercorns, dried fenugreek leaves, turmeric
powder, *garam masala* powder, lemon juice,
salt and saffron threads in a bowl and mix
well. Add the roasted gram flour and mix well.
Add the *paneer* and toss gently and marinate
for ten to fifteen minutes.

❸ Arrange the vegetables and *paneer* on satay
sticks in the following order: onion, *paneer*,
green capsicum, red capsicum, *paneer*, onion.
Prepare the remaining satay sticks similarly.

❹ Heat a shallow non-stick pan, drizzle
the remaining oil and place the satay sticks
on it. Cook on medium heat, turning the satay
sticks from time to time so that the *paneer*
pieces are cooked evenly all around.

❺ Serve hot with mint chutney.

Attractive food breaks the ice at any party
and starters are the most important to set
the pace... this skewered presentation works
wonders.

soya burger

Ingredients

1 cup soya granules
2½ cups skimmed milk
4-5 medium potatoes, boiled and mashed
1 medium onion, finely chopped
2 green chillies, finely chopped
2 tablespoons chopped fresh coriander
¼ teaspoon cumin powder
1 teaspoon red chilli powder
¼ teaspoon clove powder
¼ teaspoon cinnamon powder
1½ teaspoons lemon juice
Salt to taste
¾ cup brown breadcrumbs, for coating

To serve
4 brown burger buns
4 tablespoons mustard paste
4 tablespoons tomato ketchup
10-12 lettuce leaves
1 medium onion, sliced into rings

Method

❶ Soak the soya granules in two cups of milk for fifteen minutes. Drain and squeeze out extra milk. Grind to make finer granules.

❷ In a large mixing bowl, mix together the soya granules, mashed potatoes, onion, green chillies, fresh coriander, cumin powder, chilli powder, clove powder, cinnamon powder, lemon juice and salt.

❸ Divide the mixture into four equal-sized balls. Shape each ball into a patty of three inches diameter and about half an inch thick.

❹ Coat each patty evenly with breadcrumbs.

❺ Heat a non-stick pan and cook the patties on both sides till crisp.

❻ Halve a burger bun horizontally. Apply mustard paste on the base half and tomato ketchup on the top half. Place two to three lettuce leaves on the base half. Place the patty on this, top with onion rings, cover with the top half of the bun and serve immediately. Similarly make the remaining burgers.

Kids have a special love for burgers which are normally regarded as junk food. The soya burger is not the same because the soya provides protein, calcium and Vitamins A, B and C. The lettuce adds fibre.

kali mirch tikka

Ingredients

½ kilogram boneless chicken, skin removed and cut into 1½-inch cubes
12-15 black peppercorns, roasted and coarsely powdered
1 inch ginger
6-8 garlic cloves
2-3 green chillies
2 tablespoons olive oil
4 medium onions, sliced
1 cup drained skimmed milk yogurt
1½ tablespoons low-fat cream
1 tablespoons cornflour
1 egg white
½ teaspoon *garam masala* powder
Salt to taste
¼ teaspoon green cardamom powder
1 medium green capsicum, seeded and cut into 1-inch pieces

To serve
2 medium onions, cut into fine rings
Mint Chutney (Vol. 5, page 65), as required

Method

❶ Grind the ginger, garlic and green chillies to a fine paste.

❷ Heat one tablespoon oil in a non-stick *kadai* and sauté the onions till brown. Cool and grind to a paste.

❸ In a large bowl, combine the onion paste, drained yogurt, cream, cornflour, egg white, ginger-garlic-green chilli paste, *garam masala* powder, peppercorns, salt and cardamom powder.

❹ Add the chicken cubes and capsicum pieces, mix well and allow to marinate for one hour preferably in a refrigerator.

❺ Preheat an oven to 180°C/350°F/Gas Mark 4.

❻ Thread the chicken cubes and capsicum pieces alternately on a skewer and cook in the preheated oven at 240°C/475°F/Gas Mark 9 for fifteen minutes basting occasionally with the remaining oil.

❼ Serve hot with the onion rings and mint chutney.

Kali Mirch Tikka is a *kabab*, but with a different taste. Succulent, creamy and bite-sized, these *kababs* have a distinct peppery flavour that are a sure hit at every party. You can cook this *tikka* in an oven with a minimum amount of fat. Low-fat cream also keeps the fat content under control and helps prevent heart disease.

sichuan prawns

Ingredients

16 medium prawns, shelled and deveined

2 tablespoons red chilli paste

3 tablespoons tomato sauce

1 tablespoon soy sauce

¼ cup rice wine (optional)

¼ teaspoon MSG (optional)

2 teaspoons sugar

Salt to taste

2 cups Fish or Chicken stock (Vol. 5, page 66)

2 tablespoons oil

3-4 dried red chillies, broken

6-8 Sichuan peppers

1 inch ginger, chopped

6-8 garlic cloves, chopped

2 spring onions with greens, chopped

3 tablespoons cornflour, dissolved
in 1 cup water

1 medium green capsicum, seeded and
cut into 1-inch pieces

1 tablespoon vinegar

Method

❶ Mix the red chilli paste, tomato sauce, soy sauce, rice wine, MSG, sugar and salt to taste in one cup of stock.

❷ Heat the oil in a non-stick wok or a pan, add the chillies, Sichuan peppers, ginger and garlic and stir-fry briefly. Add the spring onions (reserving the greens for garnishing) and continue to stir-fry for a minute more.

❸ Add the prawns and cook for a minute or until the prawns turn white, stirring and tossing continuously. Add the sauce and spice mix and the remaining stock and bring it to a boil.

❹ Stir in the dissolved cornflour, add the capsicum and cook for two to three minutes or until the sauce coats the prawns. Stir in the vinegar and serve hot, garnished with spring onion greens.

The name comes from the use of Sichuan peppers in this recipe. These are not hot or pungent in taste like chillies or pepper but have a unique flavour and aroma. Only the seeds are used, the husks are removed and discarded. Konkanis would identify with it as it is very like *tirphal*.

boti kabab

Ingredients

½ kg boneless lean mutton,
cut into 1-inch cubes
2 tablespoons unripe papaya paste
1 tablespoon ginger paste
1 tablespoon garlic paste
½ teaspoon red chilli powder
¼ teaspoon garam masala powder
½ teaspoon green chilli paste
Salt to taste
2 tablespoons melted butter

Method

❶ Mix together the unripe papaya paste, ginger paste, garlic paste, chilli powder, *garam masala* powder, green chilli paste and salt. Rub the mixture over the mutton. And marinate in a refrigerator for three to four hours.

❷ Pressure-cook the marinated mutton with one cup of water till the pressure is released four times (four whistles) or till half-done. Remove the lid when the pressure has reduced completely and cook till all the moisture has evaporated.

❸ Heat a grill and grill the mutton till completely cooked. Baste with melted butter from time to time to prevent the mutton from drying out.

❹ When cooked, remove onto a plate and serve with onion *lachcha* and mint chutney.

Lean mutton is rich in protein and low in carbohydrates. Unripe papaya is not only a tenderiser but also aids in digestion.

spicy moroccan wraps

Ingredients

4 cornmeal or wholewheat tortillas
1 large green zucchini, cut into ½ inch cubes
2 medium yellow capsicums, seeded and
cut into ½ inch squares
2 tablespoons olive oil
¼ teaspoon paprika flakes
Salt to taste
¼ teaspoon black pepper powder
¼ teaspoon mixed herbs
10-12 chopped olives
½ cup sundried tomatoes, soaked in water
and chopped
1 tablespoon chopped fresh parsley

Harrisa sauce

6 whole dried red chillies
1 teaspoon coriander seeds
1 teaspoon caraway seeds
1 teaspoon cumin seeds
1 garlic clove, minced
1 tablespoon vinegar
Salt to taste

Method

❶ To make the harrisa sauce, soak the red chillies in one cup of water for ten minutes.

❷ Dry roast the coriander seeds, caraway seeds and cumin seeds till fragrant and grind them with the red chillies. Transfer the mixture into a bowl, add garlic, vinegar and salt and mix well.

❸ Preheat an oven to 180°C/350°F/Gas Mark 4.

❹ Marinate the zucchini and yellow capsicums in a mixture of olive oil, paprika, salt, black pepper powder and mixed herbs for ten minutes.

❺ Roast the vegetables in the preheated oven for twenty minutes.

❻ Add the olives, sundried tomatoes and parsley to the roasted vegetables and mix. Stir in the harrisa sauce.

❼ Spread the mixture equally over the tortillas and roll them up.

❽ Serve immediately.

Take a hint from the name. If it is too spicy for you, reduce the number of chillies. Wholewheat tortillas are better than those made with refined flour, as they are high in dietary fibre.

shawarma

Ingredients

4 chicken breasts, skinned
4 pita breads
2 tablespoons olive oil
Salt to taste

Yogurt sauce
1 cup skimmed milk yogurt
Salt to taste
1 teaspoon garlic paste
2 tablespoons lemon juice
1 sprig fresh parsley

Salad
1 medium onion, sliced
1 medium tomato, sliced
2 jalapeños, sliced
Salt to taste
2 tablespoons *tahini*
3 tablespoons skimmed milk yogurt
6-8 fresh mint leaves, torn by hand

Method

❶ Preheat an oven to 200°C/400°F/Gas Mark 6.

❷ Slit the chicken breasts lengthways without cutting through. Drizzle oil over them, sprinkle salt and fold the pieces. Thread the pieces onto a skewer. Keep the skewer on a rotating rack. Place the rack in the preheated oven and cook.

❸ For the yogurt sauce add the salt and garlic paste to the yogurt and whisk well. Add the lemon juice and mix. Place this mixture over a piece of muslin kept over a bowl, gather the edges and squeeze tight to get smooth yogurt sauce. Garnish with a sprig of parsley. Set it aside.

❹ Once the chicken is cooked, remove from the oven and shred it finely on the skewer.

❺ Toast the pita breads lightly. Slit them open to form a pocket. Set aside.

❻ Mix the onion, tomato, jalapeños, salt, *tahini*, yogurt and mint leaves to make the salad.

❼ Stuff the pita pocket with some of the shredded chicken mixture and then top it up with the salad

❽ Serve immediately with yogurt sauce.

A fast-food staple in the Middle East, Shawarma is becoming popular worldwide. *Tahini* is a paste of sesame seeds and is rich in calcium.

tandoori pomfret

Ingredients

2 (300 grams each) pomfrets
Salt to taste
2 tablespoons lemon juice
1 inch ginger
5-6 garlic cloves
½ teaspoon carom seeds
¾ cup skimmed milk yogurt
1 egg
2 tablespoons gram flour
½ teaspoon turmeric powder
1 teaspoon *garam masala* powder
2 tablespoons olive oil/rice bran oil

Method

❶ Make incisions on the pomfrets and rub in the salt and lemon juice. Set aside for twenty minutes. Grind the ginger and garlic to a fine paste.

❷ Mix together the ginger-garlic paste, carom seeds, yogurt, egg, gram flour, turmeric powder and *garam masala* powder. Rub the mixture over the fish and leave to marinate for about one hour in a refrigerator.

❸ Preheat an oven to 180°C/350°F/Gas Mark 4.

❹ Thread each pomfret onto a skewer and cook it in the preheated oven or in a moderately hot *tandoor* for about eight to ten minutes.

❺ Baste with the oil and cook in the oven/*tandoor* for another three minutes.

❻ Serve hot with lemon wedges.

Pomfrets are low in carbohydrates and high in proteins, selenium and Vitamins A and E. They are a good source of antioxidants and therefore good for maintaining a healthy heart and a clear and glowing complexion.

healthy
cornflakes bhel

Ingredients

2 cups cornflakes

1 large potato, boiled and diced

1 medium onion, chopped

1 large cucumber, seeded and diced

1 large tomato, seeded and diced

1 cup pomegranate kernels

Salt to taste

1 teaspoon *chaat masala*

2 tablespoons unripe mango, chopped

2 tablespoons chopped fresh coriander

2 teaspoons lemon juice

Method

❶ In a large bowl, combine the potato, onion, cucumber, tomato, pomegranate, salt, *chaat masala* and unripe mango and toss well to mix.

❷ Add the cornflakes, fresh coriander and lemon juice and toss again to mix well.

❸ Transfer the *bhel* to a serving bowl and serve immediately.

Whoever says that *bhel* can be made only with puffed rice will be proved wrong with this one! Cornflakes *bhel* is crunchy and small children will simply love it. What I like best about this *bhel* is that there is no fuss in preparing it. I miss the green mango when not in season, but not so much that I would give this snack a miss!